Forgive Us Our Happiness

The Katharine Bakeless Nason Literary Publication Prizes

The Bakeless Literary Prizes are sponsored by the Bread Loaf Writers' Conference of Middlebury College to support the publication of first books. The manuscripts are selected through an open competition and are published by the University Press of New England/Middlebury College Press.

Competition Winners in Poetry

1996
Mary Jo Bang, *Apology for Want*
JUDGE: Edward Hirsch

1997
m loncar, 66 *galaxie*
JUDGE: Garret Hongo

1998
Chris Forhan, *Forgive Us Our Happiness*
Daniel Tobin, *Where the World Is Made*
JUDGE: Ellen Bryant Voigt

CHRIS FORHAN

Chris Forhan (signature)

Forgive Us Our Happiness

A Middlebury College / Bread Loaf Book
Published by University Press of New England
Hanover and London

UNIVERSITY PRESS OF NEW ENGLAND publishes books under its
own imprint and is the publisher for Brandeis University Press, Dartmouth
College, Middlebury College Press, University of New Hampshire, Tufts
University, and Wesleyan University Press.

LIBRARY OF CONGRESS CATALOGING-IN-PUBLICATION DATA

Forhan, Chris, 1959–

   Forgive us our happiness / Chris Forhan.

      p.   cm.

   "The Katharine Bakeless Nason literary publication prizes"—p.

   ISBN 0–87451–938–1 (cloth : alk. paper). — ISBN 0–87451–919–5
(pbk. : alk. paper)

   I. Title.

PS3556.07316F6   1999

811'.54—dc21   99–19330

Middlebury College Press

University Press of New England, Hanover, NH 03755

Printed in the United States of America

5 4 3 2 1

for Rebecca

"Well, all right, then tell me what in your
opinion would be the best way for me to die?
I mean so that it would be as—virtuous as
possible. Well, tell me!"

"Pass on by us and forgive us our happiness,"
said the prince . . .

FYODOR DOSTOYEVSKY, *The Idiot*

Contents

I

Family History	3
Lament and Proposal	4
Something or Other	5
Reading for Pleasure	6

To Faint Forth Tearfully   7

The New World   8

The Old Sense   9

The States We Knew in School and Now Are Driving Through   10

An Honest Forest   12

Slightly, Inevitably, as a Wave   13

A Dog's Game   14

Absolution   16

Song   17

O.K. Fine   18

II

The Workings of the Internal Combustion Engine   21

Done with It   22

A Sickly Child   24

Coming To   26

Yes, Well   27

Good Boy   28

Cracking Open   29

What Furniture Means   30

Ginger Cake   31

What the Earth Knows   32

The Taste of Wild Cherry   33

Bits and Pieces   35

Night Construction   36

Elegy   37

Reprisal   38

Then Again   39

The Woman Who Could Not Wear a Hat   40

The Church of the Backyard   41

Resignation   43

III

Without Presumptions   47

Assent to Winter   48

As Columbus Would Have It, the Earth Like a Pear   50

Testimony   51

Borrowed Angels   52

Panorama without a View   53

Big Jigsaw   54

Always This Droning When I Come Calling   55

Sanctum Sanctorum   57

The Vastness. The Distant Twinkling   58

But Look Where Sadly the Poor Wretch Comes Reading   59

Land Edged by Water   60

River   61

Against Summer   62

The Garden I'm Given   63

Notes   65

Acknowledgments   67

Family History

Out of the womb of God, she ran off. We,
conceived in the muck the rain and her
wake-dust made, her eight score children,
rubbed our eyelids, licked the birth blood
off each other's faces, stood
and split into equal tribes to find her.

Over the goat-strewn hills we wandered,
over the dawn-lit cliffs and meadows,
along the marshes dotted with sedge,
begetting in gardens of larkspur and jasmine,
begetting in damp caves, boat bottoms, back
of some crumbling castle, our fall night's fire low.

Now we are many, and stumble often
across each other in drugstore lines
or hunched on separate barstools, wolf's hair
slicked down, eyeing each other sideways,
each of us hugging the narrow cage
of his body, guarding his own lost cause.

Lament and Proposal

Nobody weeps anymore over fresh graves.
Nobody's picking flowers for the dead or the living
and the near-dead yawn and spit from their hospital windows.

No one goes marrying spring around here
plucking sprigs of barberry
and, bending, launching them onto a pond ripple.

No one goes swallowing the secret word
and prowling the rain-black streets all night
feeling prescient and haunted.

Only a solemn old man now and then
hauls up the latest heap of books and drawings
to his rooftop, and sets them blazing.

The children brush their teeth with gunpowder
and clean their nails
with the nightingale's wee bones.

The wind doesn't whisper
names anymore, not even its own. So few
stars left, nobody counts them.

People are left alone to think.
They take their own word as gospel
and pray by shaking their balled-up fists.

In short: I strip and deliver myself
trembling, new, to the public pool
and ask to be baptized in the local fashion.

Something or Other

Thumb. Beryllium. Winch
and pulley. Wren. Philodendron.
Roman arch. Gila monster.
Sacred heart. The world's
unspeakable, but someone named it.

It's late. Our rickety words are eased
by tentative gestures: shrugs,
lifted palms, lead-lidded
blinks for which we could,
if cornered, deny intent.

Still. Still. The waves rake
the beach, reach our naked feet
and wake us—then
the brain flails, we
gaze, transfixed:

These foaming rows . . .
This blue fused with white . . .
This light, this mute assertion . . .
Something or other. An absence. Nothing.
Mediterranean is too long a word.

Reading for Pleasure

In bed a hundred years. Rumpled sheets. My lush
and utter sloth. Every moment glows: a fine flame
ascending, circling, sinking at last in the soot

of all my blissful squandered hours. Walls of books.
Pages dog-eared, dawdled over. Another big book
of life in my lap, lamplit page like ivory, every

word a whisper in the next one's ear, a lovesick sigh. Gone
my elbow's itch, my ankle's ache, the fly that hummed
and bumped the glass. Only clarity. Just my blood

hushed in its steady work. At the far edge of the city, a barberpole
winds down, screels to a stop. The last sound. Now
the essential abides, the world aligned, languid: a plain

cooled by moonlight. Stalks of wheat. A shuttered house.
A Dodge on blocks. A barn. A cow, asleep.
In its heart, a book, pages riffling.

To Faint Forth Tearfully

And when particulars won't suffice: Rain
spotting a packed dirt driveway. Some
lame mutt's scarred and withered tail.

A swallow's nest in an old woodpile.
A soiled bootlace, sun-baked, brittle,
that snaps in your fist and falls limp—

chin on your chest, of a sudden
you're genuflecting, humbled
in the presence of your own ineptness.

Winter: The curled-up aspen leaves
neither skate nor whimper, wind-flung
over the crusted surface of the frozen lake.

There is little human in any of this—
little in the sure arrival of winter,
little of you in the leaves or wind

or in the unreflective lake. For this
you're trusted to faint forth tearfully,
hymns of praise on your trembling lips.

A couch spring rips the worn upholstery:
Dull, ungainly, strange, like
you, it exhibits itself—it

exists, like you, in the present moment
equally helpless to know itself, only
you're the one doing all the thinking.

The New World

"The seas all cross'd, weather'd the capes, the voyage done..."

WALT WHITMAN

Our luggage is packed. There's no place to go.
Our old and broken travelers' hearts are watching
the last train grind away from the station,
lose steam, and rust on the tracks. We talk

but nothing's left to explain, except ourselves,
which is why we keep changing the subject,
why no one can speak of the moon anymore,
at least without self-mocking humor.

Too long, Walt, "by the bivouac's fitful flame."
Too long by the edge of the sluiceway,
not much golden on the opposite bank
to gaze at—only a herd of us, turning back

with no good schools ahead or affordable
haircuts or passage to the next world, which,
we gather, was merely a gleaming mirage. The groaning
ships that brought us have taken on water

and sunk. A comforting story is being
constructed of this, though for the present
we sleep beneath the inalterable stars
and twitch and lash, like shackled dancers.

The Old Sense

It wasn't as if we'd lost the magic
formula, the one that had always emboldened us,
steeped as it was in the black beginnings

of time, passed in the blood to us,
our needful burden, our only means
of turning the battered earth into song.

It wasn't as if the incantation
were remembered wrong after all
these years—years in which the moon

tore itself loose from the pine's spiked branches
to drift indifferently overhead,
years in which the seed astir

in winter's pocket, and the early rose,
turned out to have no particular meaning
touching ourselves. Tonight, though,

as the wicks were lit, the cruet
filled to the lip, the heavy sack
split, the ashes strewn—the sky flashed

a few ruined stars. Among the gathered, someone
coughed and wound his watch. We conjured
nothing, straining to awaken

the old sense of inevitability and reverence,
our fathers' words were ghosts in our mouths
and the fish lay dead in our hands.

The States We Knew in School and Now Are Driving Through

Riddle of gullies, hills, orchards
fat with apples, fields of melons
swollen in the sun. God
must be trying to win our attention
again with concrete things.
The best such thing is a long
car, if it's moving,
windows rolled up, radio on,
single index finger resting
on the bottom arc of the steering wheel,
billboards blazing up at road's edge,
stucco motor lodges sporting
rose-hued pools and the names
of dead Indians. All around,
the states we knew in school and now
are driving through: the Keystone
and the Show Me states; some place
over the morning fields, the Windy City,
shoulders heaving; somewhere, Denver,
mountain town, spurs glinting
silver in the sun. Shimmering
under the cool waters of the Chippewa
ride the muskellunge, state fish
of Wisconsin. The continent
we studied once in rows is rolling
under us, road signs showing the way
to Lincoln, Pierre, Topeka,
Santa Fe, each with its earnest
houses of assembly
determining irrigation policy
or a new state bird. Seaward,

the brawny rivers surge:
Columbia, Missouri, Colorado,
producing hydroelectric power
for grocers storing frozen chicken
and salesmen penciling in their itineraries
helped by the solemn illumination
of hotel lamps. So much to see,
so much to drive by: tumbled shacks
of the curious poor, an open truck
of migrant laborers, laughing,
though the sound can't reach us.
All the way west, we keep our eyes
forward, judging how far we've come
by the gnats who've hurled themselves
at the windshield. Then, whether
we enter the sky train, riding
its wrist-thick cable to scale
some peak, or enter the theme park's
watery tunnel on tracks, we give up
our ticket for a place in the car:
the snug belt, the familiar
thunk of the door locks.

An Honest Forest

Enter the blackest woods: a mute, brooding forest
on the farthest northern edge of an otherwise
barren continent—you enter, of course,
the pure, unalterable, mud-thick, root-scarred
depths of yourself, dropping crumbs, creeping close
to the cool, unmoving first flame. Enter an honest forest

and nothing happens. Stray patches of sun
gleam on the leaves. There are ferns
and squirrels. You go in alive and come out
a little hungry, your watch heavy on your wrist,
a pine needle lodged in your collar, a stone
in your boot. Not much there to witness—

just atoms persisting in their tedious work
as anywhere: seedlings straining their brainless
bodies, crowded by elders who shrug
their dumb limbs—some of them, weakened, leaning
toward one another, whispering rumors,
the rest of them rotting standing up.

Slightly, Inevitably, as a Wave

Don't try. Spiny shrubs beget
fat raspberries, wild in spring, dangling—
brushed once, perhaps, by a passing
flicker's wing—then split by rain
in August, left to rot, or stain
the deft hornet's tongue. Don't

try. The bright boy who mouths vowels,
leaning over the kitchen table,
fingers rigid, tracing
the unfamiliar letters with his crayon,
looks up from his work: dazed, graying,
crouched on the curb, arthritic,
pages of old newspaper
crammed in his coat for warmth—
jabbering at ghosts. Don't try.

Or: Try slightly, inevitably, as a wave
breaks, as a frayed rope unravels—

as a weighty organ note travels
upward, circling, dispersing
into the chapel rafters,
as stained glass cracks the light,
as a few friends shuffling along below
pause, then ease
the long coffin around the door jamb.

A Dog's Game

Packed dirt, back of the shed. I dig
close to where the dog has done his digging
(damn him), shifting dirt to fill his holes. Oh

game of displacement, you're a dog's game
I'm caught in, a dim-wit's mission, this
tilting the earth toward my desire.

I level the ground as flat as Sunday's
flickering final light will allow. My too-long
hair's in my eyes, already

a trickle of sweat on my brow. Such
hunched work hurts—a hint
of an ache in my back and wrist,

already a blister
insinuating itself in the groove
between left thumb and forefinger. Clink

at the tip of my shovel. Not
a rock—something rounder, hollow, white,
too white to remain in the ground.

I stoop, loosen it, tap the dirt away.
The size of an egg. Not an egg:
a teapot, gleaming porcelain, fit

to fill a thimble to the brim—
a piece from a child's tea set, lost
or left behind in who knows what

long gone year—here, in the middle
of nowhere, just where I'd find it.
I set it in my palm, its small, certain weight.

Someone else held this toy, then felt
the ground shift, attention slip,
and left it here: a gift

to be lifted out of the past and onto
this present fencepost, to catch
the day's last ragged light.

I lean on the shovel above
my half-done work. I call it
good enough. What pure, yearned-for thing

exceeds what chance delivers clumsily
into the hands: impractical, real
as a buried toy? What howl now

or yawp of joy would I not
claim as mine—I, whose habit
is to long for a soul

without a body, its hair disheveled,
boots blackened by dirt, oh blessed
imperfectible earth, oh happy accident.

Absolution

Man is good. What else would he be?
The low April light lifts
tendrils, curls of new green
twining almost imperceptibly
up the fence slat. The burglar

holds his breath, steadying
the gate latch between thumb
and finger, then gently, as if
with affection, lifts it
while the family sleeps. Let

all sleep. Let the last
leaves lose their grip, let them
twist toward earth in the unplanned dance
that is their nature. A man will dance
and at times will choose not to speak

when spoken to, as the badger digs deep
and the busy-brained acorn keeps
its weighty secret. Let me
keep my secret. Let me dawdle,
admiring the moons of my fingernails.

Let me refuse to seek my better nature,
to strain toward the edge of things,
scouring plains, scaling cliffs,
just to find a pond to gaze at, just to
bring back a turtle I can put in my pocket.

Song

Must we sing of the dead again? Yes—
and ruined leaves, fever-tinged, thinning
twists of river, boughs quivering
when the ripe pear drops, braided hours
unraveling, stale moonlight—the old

peculiarities. Shake a small tree, it will mutter
a platitude. Kneel at grave's edge, your moans
meld with the moans of the dead, and both dissolve
in the droning wind. But we keep our distance. We sing
of the end as if astounded. Each day

is improbable, a horse we can't trust, riderless,
galloping past us, gold-stitched saddle
agleam in the slanting light—
ragged anguished clouds above it
fleeing like deposed tyrants. We cannot stop

the roots of the juniper crumbling
a bit of pavement at the churchyard's edge.
Our porches sag. Each ocean wave has its own
bleak imperative—and the smoke of burning woods
and the mouse lost in the snow, far from the nest.

The dead shall not rise. The leaves shall repeat
their one trick, needing no consolation.
We sing, needing consolation, praising
things that change so we may
live among them cheerful strangers.

O.K. Fine

Forgive us our happiness, forgive us
our wacky haircuts, the way we thirst for success
as TV evangelists and high school typing teachers,

letting the crow go silent for want of attention
to his dreary mystery, turning our backs to the sea
repeating unweariedly its one empty gesture.

Forgive us the way we inherited this hallowed ground
and set up shop along the border, avoiding
the dank interior, the way we labor

instructing each other on proper storage
of household combustibles, swapping thoughts
on butter substitutes, wrench sets, sealants,

bleach-based smudge removers—all things solid
by which we're comforted, the way we talk and talk and guard
our hearts, our pure and idiot middle, believing

life is a gift to earn by not letting on
our desire for it. This is O.K. This is fine.
We're plenty astonished. Summer's come, shuffling in

like a laid-off textile worker. Radio towers
rise like pines through the mist behind
the convenience store. Its white sign

stutters on as dawn arrives, tipping
its lavender hat, settling a light on each pelican
lawn ornament and pink concrete garden frog.

There's always something. The frocked bishop wiggling, relieving
an itch. A doll's arm gnawed by a dog at the edge
of the park. A wig in the road. We're plenty astonished.

We are at work on the past to make the future

More bearable.

MARK STRAND

The Workings of the Internal Combustion Engine

Because I resemble too nearly the men and women I'm not,
Because their kind of thought is too familiar and not familiar enough,
So I study my shoes if we should pass on the sidewalk;

Because I'm able to chat with Orville, Pete, and Chester for minutes
    on end
Concerning the workings of the internal combustion engine
And nobody blinks, nobody dares to listen to the moment stall and
    sink into silence;

Because I interrupt and order coffee to disguise that I have lost the
    train of the conversation
And then if I should take a sip must do so out of trust
That Lily, the waitress, hasn't laced it with cyanide;

Because I hunch tight-lipped among others in an elevator car,
    feigning nonchalance,
But feeling the sudden weight of our oafishness,
Winking when a stranger winks and then having to guess at the
    exchange's significance;

Because my mother calls me son and I wonder what she's really
    saying,
I waste my days beyond the city limits, hunting through caves and
    ditches,
Stumbling over rare flowers, naming them after the people I love.

Done with It

At the county landfill, a scavenging grackle,
in luminous purple-black cowl,
eyeing me with the indifference reserved
for those of his order. I have come

to disown my sofa—worn, gone weak
in the middle, a battered cabinet
I strained to lift, a sack of clothes,
a box of books—things I thought

I loved and gathered strength from,
meager harbors where I anchored
in my languor, in my sleepy
certainty, and woke up stranded.

I will stand above these things
and speak no words, but watch
a derelict shoe go back
to the self it was without me,

watch the long yellow sleeve of a shirt
wave in the wind, useless, bright
with the sheen of abandonment.
I will learn to live with fragments:

clumps of kite string trapped in branches,
clatter of a tin can kicked
down a rain-slick alley—shreds
of memory, little things

that cling without my clinging to them:
pennies trembling on the track, a black
pebble from the roof of the house
I grew up in, the sly

advance of the elm tree's shade
toward the rail fence in autumn, chill
of my first snow, sidewalk slush,
red boots my mother tugged on my feet,

or lying in bed as a boy, August,
the room buzzing with dusk and sudden
silence, scent of sweet upturned dirt
as the curtains swelled and sank.

I will serve what served me well, far back,
and pick through the old scraps, rapt
in a faithful watchfulness. It is time
to make my movements count

like the grackle, who, in his hunger,
in his solitude, as I come
too near, lifts his wings
and shrieks just once.

A Sickly Child

Loosed from the womb, I swooned
on my first breath. The doctor
urged me into this world
with a kiss to my still lips.

Each of my bristling sisters
slipped her skates off and tiptoed
in stocking feet to pass my door.
I was given much medicine
from large blue bottles.

The blinds were always drawn
and my windows cracked an inch
in summer. Often I drowsed,
the dull sound of weeping or whispering
in the hall, or one of my brothers
calling my name from the darkening street.

Grandmother, wigged and recoiling
from the stench, occasionally entered
my room at Christmas, leaving me
big books to prop on my chest.
Legends of the living dead.
Adventures of a sightless orphan
and his mongrel dog. Tales
of the martyred child saints.

Also, sometimes, late afternoons—mother
stooped in the kitchen, straining a cauldron
of steaming soup for me; father
alone in the basement stuffing
swansdown into immense pillows
for my bed—I'd slip out
to the neighbor kid's, Eddie O'Shaughnessy,
who'd beat me bloody
and tell me to get over it.

Coming To

Thought boxed my ears when I was born. It took me years
to come to. Ringed with summer blooms, I sat
in the backyard swing, gripping the chains,

calculating the sum and force of swings I'd need
to reach a tolerable height that would bring
the fastest fall. Today, I will not sing

of my common heart, its dumb, aging tedium. Once
I knew a planet: small, blue, silvered
around the edges. I would not call it mine.

Bored, lurching from the swing, waving gnats away,
I stumbled, bruising both shins on a stump cloaked
by wild grasses. Fearing in my pain

to suck the honeyed air too deep, I sat
still in the back of the family Buick, puzzling
over each moment that passed like a chattering gadget.

Amid the fallen twigs and gravel, small toads leaped.
Swallows dipped and skittered. The caterpillar
raised his shimmering tent high in the cherry branches.

The bright-leafed sycamore flashed in the breeze. Far
across the valley, storm clouds glowered, then turned back,
trailing their purplish skirts beneath them.

Giver, lover of things, whatever listened then
and still is listening: Forgive me. I would not budge.
I held my breath as if that joy were a hornet.

Yes, Well

I learned to talk by accident.
Under my breath at the hunt I said *Oxbow.*
Pieshell. Eloise. Peccary. Tinfoil.
The words just flowered up like—
not like flowers, really—actually,
they didn't so much flower
as arrive from out of me without permission.
It couldn't be called a talent, or gift—
condition, maybe, though that sounds clinical.
Even my mother was surprised by my eloquence.
When I first whispered *Mama* her jaw dropped
as if she'd fallen from a cliff
which I'd think would be terrifying.

Good Boy

These are the shoes I remove at the doorstep.
This is the shirt I return to the drawer.
This is the sink where I draw the dishwater.
These are the cups and plates I dry.

This is the way I sit all day
in the parlor, watching the tangled vines
rise up around me, and the forest darken,
watching myself bend low toward the river
to drink, watching six black bears
slouch up to greet me and kiss my forehead.

This is my mother, patient beside me,
waiting to fill my bowl with soup.
This is the way I bow my head
to pray. These are my two small hands,
scrubbed and scrubbed of all but their true name.

Cracking Open

Every morning it goes like this:

Hans, I say, toss me that overcoat,
toss me my thick skin.
Last night my bones were cold again.

My sister in the next room, stiffening
her mop-handled spine
against the locked door.

Even the staircase unable to squeak,
forks and knives
in bundles in a long drawer.

But today: a sparrow, her chirp
in our tall tree.

And now: the cook
churning supper from the rag bucket—

father and mother, alone
at the table, chuckling about
some recurring nightmare.

What Furniture Means

That the table and lamp have no need for me
is unimportant. It's that others
who turn on the lamp to read by
have no need for me, except
for the use of the lamp.

My brother clears my papers from the table
and sets down his plate.
When he finishes eating he'll plan
how to dismantle the table
and build my coffin.

Ginger Cake

The cool, the shadowy hour, supper
bubbling in the upstairs pan, winter
flicking soft flakes at the pane.
Our Father, who art in heaven . . .

I'm the little boy who knows
the last inch of my room
and mother's kitchen—I finish
my sister's sentences.

I read the books that once were read
to me: a girl who sings, high
in her tower, braiding her heavy hair;
a long oven, big as a witch.

Whatever falls upon our tongues
we speak here, and then forget.
Only our two thin cats decline
to talk, having tongues like spoons

to scoop the milk, to swallow all
their idle vowels down with it,
swallowing all they could tell
of this tale, and what comes next:

How our pale, humble-hearted
Christ stoops to extend his hand,
how a grinning hag offers a bit
of ginger cake, and I take it.

What the Earth Knows

In August's grinding heat I sit
among dahlias with my insolent sister,
backs against the garden wall, bare legs
outstretched, dusty, scratched
from kneeling, yanking weeds out
by their prickly roots. Well,
any adult who cared to look
could tell we've done our share of work.
Ten and nine and otherwise pleased
to play on this earth, we were set to work
by Dad: a bucket of weeds by lunch,
the dirt around the roses hoed.
Done, we don't budge. We're going to feel
misunderstood, we're going to curse
our friends, surely riding bikes,
surely rafting, collecting tadpoles.
Even with snake-tongued tools, stabbing
the ground, even with thoughts of crying,
we couldn't make most weeds give up:
long, tough as rubber, they held
or snapped off quick in our fists. Now
the garden's thick with gnats and hot
and I will not set a snail upon
my sister's shoulder. I will not whisper
that she is the adopted child
discovered asleep in a gopher hole
and she will not rejoice in my large ears
or in my knobby knees. Something
is making us sit unmoved together,
smelling the upturned earth and the juice
of the bitter weeds on our hands,
learning what the earth knows:
an agreeable intransigence.

The Taste of Wild Cherry

for Kevin and Dana

The weight of the moment: immeasurable, the weight
of the self, of Dad's glance backward at us kids
shrieking and grappling in mid-winter's backseat.

At issue: a last stick of gum. At issue:
the misperception of a gesture's intent—
the insinuating jerk of someone's shoulder

sideways, the curl of an upper lip, my sour
sister's scowl, my brother's love
of torture games, my own forebearance

in the face of unrelieved suffering. I'm writing
the scene as it happens, seeking
from light and shadow the permanence of stone,

permanence of the snapped-shut ashtray that traps
smoke from Dad's smoldering cigarette. We're traveling
somewhere, the day has a name and weather, traffic

surrounds us, each car with its purpose, but I'm
intent on my sister's hair, getting a good grip,
eyeing her fist that filched the gum, my free arm

shielding my head from my brother's blows. I note
his wolfish laughter, an ache piercing my ribs,
my sister's willed, mechanical tears, my own

quiet call to God for justice. Dad's
pulled the car off the road. Faceless,
he turns, snarling words I won't recall.

My mind's on the gum he demands and slips
in his pocket, wild cherry, my mind's
on the flavor it should have had in my mouth.

I'm forging my note to the future, recording
all I know of this moment before
the moment completes itself: pearls of rain

on the windows, scent of wet carpet, song
on the radio fading—I'm saving
this one thing, nothing, smoke in my hands.

Bits and Pieces

Streetlamp glint on my watch, a Christmas gift, I'm ten, the tin
   wristband pinches my skin, my sister calls again from the kitchen
   window, it's getting late,
I sit on the cool clay of the empty driveway, knees pulled in to my
   chest, I'm eight, I'm making a pact with myself—"Never forget," a
   cat, skulking, lean, passes his orange-white length along my ankle,
   that thing I vowed to remember, what was it?
Sun on my face, sun on the wide water, bow of a rowboat, I might be
   five, wooden cross-bench worn and hot beneath my bare thighs,
   oarlocks clunking behind me, who holds the oars?
The Ford has a flat, I help my father fix it, we kneel in an arc of light
   in the lumberyard, I'm three weeks into the second grade, a mist
   of rain moistens the lug wrench resting in my open palm,
Stretched on a mossy pond bank, beyond a gully a block from home,
   I plunge my arm in the green-black murk up to the elbow, urging
   a tadpole into my mayonnaise jar, on the street above me a cement
   truck slows, wheezes, downshifting,

Only these few scenes gleaming in the cave of the past, only these
   chipped hieroglyphics, as if hints of some other steady
   underneath-it-all self, undiscoverable, hushed,
Or maybe the spider I startled in the washtub, twisting the spigot that
   morning in one of my early summers, means nothing, and the
   memory of it now means nothing,
Why think still of the way that spider circled the drain—or the day,
   studying snails and rotting leaves beneath the side porch, I found
   my uncle's long lost blue fedora, limp but only slightly stained?
What is it about the time the weather turned, the sky purpling
   suddenly, and I ran a mile to school ecstatic, pelted by sleet?
What was I then, what am I now, who can come to myself only in bits
   and pieces?

Night Construction

He's at it again, Dad's bumping his head
like a kite against the night sky.
He's brought up his hammer
and some tenpenny nails.
He can't seem to get the moon to stay put.

The nail heads glint in his fist.
It's Mom on the lawn with the flashlight
begging him to come to bed, Dad
grinning down, a nail between his teeth,
a slow galleon of stars sliding by.

Elegy

I was born of my father's aching back
and tottered along behind him down our one path

learning to walk by watching his shoes
hauling around his crooked shadow.

The day my father cursed the earth and took it
for his bed, I felt my own breath shorten.

I inherited his thick skull, tilted spine
crow's laugh, house, and week-long silences.

I sleep and meet him on a crowded ferry
back in this world, and he wears my face

and when I wake and stand, his hands
dangle at the ends of my arms

and when I fall and hug the earth
when I feel my own knees buckle

I pick myself up, being not my father
and think twice, being my father's son.

Reprisal

I've had to learn to love
the word *reprisal*, coming
upon me in this older age
prizelike, a punishment

the only means
to restore at last
my self—my lost, my
snow-torn rose. Late

without thought, tonguing
another loosening molar
smoothing my death suit
I woke, trembling

and unafraid.
He who robs me
must be made to feel
my loss. Then I am

like the sturdy maple
out of which is carved
my home: four corner posts
eight solid roof beams

varnished parlor floor
my absent-minded, muddy-
shoed son tramps over
and a long stick to hit him with.

Then Again

To find me, try the street of Mahoney's Fruit
and Furniture, street of the Software Barn
and the Sacred Heart Federal Credit Union,
street where opposites mix, where all the bliss
and rancor I recall, all the cluttered details
of the past, reach a happy ending, settling in
at the same address. The sun has almost finished
drying patches of last night's rain. A cat
trapped in a crawl space squirms out
through a crack in the apartment building's foundation,
stretches, purrs, and cleans herself
by the feet of a dog, dozing in the driveway.
A vagrant sits like a sultan on a ruby sofa
set out as trash near the curb. He waves.
All of my friends wave, too, as they pass
in their polished convertibles. High above the street,
behind a shade, my father and mother sleep
in their one bed, each spooling out a dream
briskly-plotted and comical. No need to wake them.
Soon they will rise and go down together
to breakfast, to the glistening pitcher of milk
that waits in the Frigidaire. I'm only riding
my bike up the block and back again, balanced
on memory's rickety wheel. No need to wake them.

The Woman Who Could Not Wear a Hat

Aunt Beryl who could not wear a hat
declined to come to Easter dinner.
Aunt Beryl come hatless come hatless we'd say
arrive with your blue curls drenched in rain
arrive amid hushed admiration of your pink suit.
Think of the raging magnolia in bloom
unbounded by hats. Aunt Beryl the honeysuckle!
Think of the bareheaded song of the meadowlark
dawn spreading hatless over the broad Atlantic.
Think of the white peaks high in the moonlight.
Consider the damp tufted head of the infant
proclaiming its entrance into our glad world.
Think of the valiant, hatless poor.
Think of the evening's dull expanse
and us, think of your miserable
nieces and nephews, fatted on goose
nursing our flat punch, stuck
telling Aunt Beryl stories
the woman who could not wear a hat.

The Church of the Backyard

Delores wears her celery-colored
swimming suit, the one embellished
with tiny slices of watermelon,
a bite out of each of them.

Assuredly seven, she's eighteen months
and one day older than Ronald, who trips
and sprawls again in the gravel. Last Tuesday
that trick earned a popsicle.

Our newly teenaged sister Vicki
suns herself and paints her toenails green
to match her plastic sandals. Starting today,
she proclaims, we are to call her Victoria.

Mother wears her summer hat: the wide
fried egg that shades her paperback
and wobbles around her ears whenever
she laughs or lifts her head to speak

to father: first one in the pool,
first time out of a business suit
all season, splayed on his inner tube,
circling the deep end, orchid-white.

I've got my Batman outfit on
and, stern-jawed, saunter across the lawn
wearing the others' admiration
lightly. Who would say

through all the little deaths, the separations,
all the long untidy years to come,
each unholy ruckus (the wine glass
smashed against the wall in anger, fists

that pound the steering wheel, bodies
sitting bolt upright in bed with night sweats),
who would say, through all of this,
we're not redeemed by our essential silliness?

Resignation

after Strand

I give back the crooked tie around my neck.

I give back my cabinet of tax returns.

I give back my corporate success, the gold shoehorn, my wages,
normal and overtime.

I give back my skill at door-to-door selling of plaster frog and
terrapin replicas.

I give back frogs and terrapins.

I give back herons and their weedy nests.

I give back my acrobatics medal, my honorable mention in dramatic
entrances.

I give back my sarcasm born of fear, my swagger and bouquet of
smiles, my swift, accidental words of hurt and comfort.

I give back my boyhood fame for my way with numbers, I give back
my way with numbers.

I give back my running leaps into clear lake water, my love of song,
sleight of hand, dimes flattened on the track, books filled with
moonlit autumn trees and horses clacking up rocky cliffs.

I give back the cave of sleep in which I believed I met the hundred
tribes of earth and heaven.

I take back the crumbs of bread I flung behind me as I went and
return them to the cupboard.

I give back summer.

I give back winter, every angel or man I formed in snow.

I give back my Christmas catapult rocket, impossible to put together.

I give back my hands, tongue, blood.

I give back my feet, curled and shamed.

I give back the ease of my first trick, crawling along the rug to reach
my mother's ankle.

I give back my first wild sobbing talk.

No one needs to know this happened.

Nothing regenerates us, or shapes us again from the dust.
Nothing whispers our name in the night.
Still must we praise you, nothing.

                    Still must we call to you.

                    CHARLES WRIGHT

Without Presumptions

The cineplex is showing a monster movie: our autobiography.
At century's end, such blunt articulation of our condition
is useful, seeing as how we're half human

and how the tale of our being exiled angels is no longer credible
though our wings, still rooted to our backs, flap loosely
and our hearts slap sadly inside our chests.

Our heads seem suddenly oddly shaped. What crown can fit us?
Our hands are the hands of apes. We sprout coarse hair
and idle sexual fears. Lately, the sky is painted

a different blue. Our stately, creaking hymns
can't bear this news. We sit and sing, roped
to the past in the midst of the perishing

present, dressed in our ancestors' threadbare clothes,
wearing their moustaches quaintly, like smudges of charcoal.
Our dumpsters overflow and smell of the day before yesterday.

Our antique gas pump and hubcap collection rusts. As the dog
adjusts to its compact, practical brain, sniffing
and shitting, we're having to find a way to live again

without presumptions—shutting the maintenance manual,
watching awhile in darkness through the picture window
pines calm beneath snowfall, old branches gathering the temporary
    weight.

Assent to Winter

1

Spring comes goat-like up the hills,
rutting, in love with itself. Honeyed
summer, drunk, as if bludgeoned
and dumped by a gang of angels,
drowses in the queasy air, assailed by flies,
then flares into autumn: doleful, talismanic,
dropping apples at our feet.

2

Winter mounts the creaky stairs
like anyone, carrying its own
clumsy coffin on its back.
Ratty coat grimed with soot,
it wheezes, slumps against the door,
then heaves its way in, stomping off
mud, slush, and bits of dead grass.

3

For oak climbing, cool mid-May is best,
and when a boy has chosen such a time
to find his tree and try the highest, slimmest branch
that still will bear his weight, as he sways
in the day's twined limbs, he is for an instant
not alone, and he knows that all things live forever.
This is true, and this is not true.

4

Beneath the frost-broken concrete sidewalks of the city lie the radiant
   bones of the dead.
The bus driver whistles, wearing his moss-green pants and shirt,
   death's uniform.
Avenues cross, marking the spot with signs inscribed with the names
   of the dead.
The florist cuts the stems of a dozen forget-me-nots, death's favorite
   flower.
The rabbi shuffles along, his phlegmy cough the traditional song of
   the dead.
Children whoop and yelp at dusk in a vacant lot, their baseball
   diamond made from the four joined points of death.
A few first flakes whirl down into the hushed city, stutter and vanish
   near a rusty barrel's trapped flame.

5

When every branch is bare
a man trudges to the center
of January's field, fresh with snow,
lies on his back, and knows,
fanning wide his arms and legs, he cannot
will himself away from his body, scraping
the earth as he waves at heaven.

As Columbus Would Have It, the Earth Like a Pear

Absurd to assume
that the whole of which
he knew but a part

would take the shape
of a thing he could pluck
and rub on his coat sleeve.

Still, famished Isabella
was given the world
on a silver plate.

Not so you, my love,
to whom I have nothing to give
but this polished apple.

Testimony

I could tell how the water stung
then swallowed me, bearing me
wholly alive and looking
to the other side.

I could tell what I knew there.

I could tell how my arms locked
crosswise against my chest
and a gnat tapped my thumbnail
twice with his hind leg.

I could tell how I wanted
to forgive God, the Devil,
and Rob McChesney,
who one day in fourth grade
stamped me with chalk-dust.

I could tell how of the three
I loved Rob McChesney.

I could tell how the water
swallowed me. I could tell
how the first touch stung
my toe, so I offered
both my ankles.

Borrowed Angels

When my skull has no thought in it, my throat no cough,
and my wrists quit itching from their snug cuffs,
and my right hand halts at last its long hello,
and my secret part returns perhaps to a place it knew
and lost, like a dog come back to a thankful master,

my words will have been the first to abandon me,
slinking back to the silence from which they'd come,
words I trusted because I uttered them, presuming
I named the way the wild plum leaf twists toward the sun
and the azalea blazes, words with which I called myself

brainless, lover of bungles, Prince of Flub, and so in time
convinced myself of my own necessity, words I spoke less
than they spoke me, so what I said well I knew imperfectly—
borrowed angels, guardians of all that's beyond me, muttering
while shrugging me off, *We've lugged this monkey long enough.*

Panorama without a View

No willow in sight. No steadfast maple, nor air
thick with shad flies or August heat. No foxglove
lining a winding stream, no girl in white on a footbridge
filling the stream with salt tears. No horizon of tawny hills
and glinting turrets. Not so much as a single acre of field,
no poor soul in the midst of it, hitching his pants up,
having to abandon himself to the rain. No lake
distant and shrouded with mist; if there were it would not be
filled with golden fish or sleek silver ones, none with pockmarks
and coarse black whiskers. No toads mocking the groans of the ill.
In the foreground—let's call it that—not enough grass for an ant
to lay down his knapsack. No ants. No mound of black soil,
no grandpa pulling the soil around him, blanket for the long night.
Ah! Not a thing of use there, no words to describe it.

Big Jigsaw

I've hunched so long above this puzzle
laid out on my gouged and ink-stained workbench,
I think, at last, it's unsolvable,
that the only meaning it holds is told
in the moments I feel on the verge
of understanding, and it turns me back.

The pieces: so small, so many. How they
belong together is beyond me,
though early on my mind inclined
toward an idyllic scene: a yellow field,
all jonquils, a sea, the wide horizon . . .

The dog's dish is empty. My wife and children
sleep. The house is hushed, except
for the stout hall clock that ticks its minutes.
Here in my patch of lamplight, time
dawdles, waiting for me to catch up,
though a few small hairs on my wrist
have gone white, and evening's blank encircles me.

Who made this puzzle? If I sought him out
would he hear my plea and reveal its logic?
But the hour is late, my vision strained.
How could I look for him now, though he were
waiting for me, and knew me by name?

Always This Droning When I Come Calling

I'm sick of my perfumed voice,
the stink of it, thick in the air.

Ma'am, you'll allow me—my pleasure,
surely—to assist with those packages?

Always this droning when I come calling,
the old warble. *Roger, it won't be said*

there are strangers here. Have
another slab of meatloaf. Sweet

sweet song, where is the room
that does not reek of you? Always

the one tune, its scent of seduction,
its forgive-me whiff. Always

my stiff cloak of self-regard
to wrap around others' shoulders.

Might not preference shown
to this pupil (I confess

my muddled thoughts do little honor
to the weight of this matter) prove

dispiriting to the other children,
as, say, Roberto or Seth?

Sick sick sick
of this fetid stench I'm swaddled in,

of words wafting into the wind,
an incantation, frightening off

the ghost of my better self, who knows
the tongue, for all its lithe movements,

is rooted, goes nowhere. So true.
My fault. Sorry to have bothered you.

Sanctum Sanctorum

I think I've lived enough now to be lonely
and be mad about it. I might as well rent out
a warehouse and sit there, scowling, every
goddamn light on, surrounded by loneliness.
I might as well hire back the angel who quit me,
spent veteran of my staying up too late
thinking. I'd make him put on some grimy
coveralls, sweep up the place now and then,
and stagger a half block, hauling the trash can
out in the rain to the empty street, and then
I'd make him come back again.

The Vastness. The Distant Twinkling

When the Great Unknowable One shook out
the immaculate tablecloth of the stars,
concealing all the while the sight
of his own magnificence, we applauded.
We kept this up for some time. What else

could we do? What words could we speak
in reply? Oh, it was past all comprehension.
The vastness. The distant twinkling. The simple
inexplicableness of the trick. Ourselves there
to witness. A wonder, we told each other, to be sure,

but with something a little sad about it.
At last, our hands numb from clapping,
each of us slipped his hat on, waved so long,
and went his solitary way. We were hungry
and we had a few things to think about.

But Look Where Sadly
the Poor Wretch Comes Reading

Spellbound, gnawing my own bones, obsessed
with the failing art of the semicolon, here
at the midpoint of life, a flicker: I'm awful

to my wife and neighbors, I'm awful to the dog,
I'm awful to harbor in my secret heart
a tale I can ravel out to myself only.

I'm awful to want to read all night,
to follow myself as I amble through black air,
pausing only to pare my fingernails

and then to forage so long in this old wood
hunched, tramping down dim trails, grubbing
for thick sticks, tufts of brownish moss

something to help this house I'm building
against the north air, against whatever
beasts slink round to steal my loneliness

here where I humble myself, where I smooth
a square in the dirt, kneel, and linger
hands on the earth, to feel below

the pulse of the roots' immense muscles, to know it
from my muffled breath—a ghost's.
A dog barks. My heart sinks. I raise

my eyes from the page: it is morning outside
and springtime. Yes, of course, it is springtime
again. The season of heat and desire.

Land Edged by Water

I'm tired of being charmed by winter,
I'm tired of gnarled limbs, sullen leaden night, pickups stuck
    churning in deep snow, headlights dimming,
I'm tired of death, the great parade, the great hymn of death,
    scythe-faced Cortez and his sun-dazed entourage,
I'm tired of land edged by water, the wearisome ever approaching
    ocean waving its promises,
I'm tired of wringing the wheel, knowing brakes fail, veering between
    the lip of the cliff and the center line,

I'm tired of more than one thing at a time, of all things emblematic:
    ashes, cradles, phone poles, willows in strong wind,
I'm tired of the wobbly desk at which I labor over this long division,
I'm tired of the priestly nodding way of roosters and the cloistered
    hen,
I'm tired of death, tired of his henchman: deathless love of
    deathlessness, shrill angel in the dumpster,
I'm tired of desire,

Tired of heaven's hill's height, the heron's flight, the luminous ripe
    orange,
Sick of bending to hear my ticking wrist,
Sick of the sleep I nightly seek and consent to,
Sick of phosphorescent summer, forest floors black and still beneath
    broad green-yellow August leaves,
Sick of sun-streaked gulls wheeling eastward over the swollen
    irreducibly blue and wordless sea, of scrambling down to the
    docks and setting my own ships ablaze to keep from sailing.

River

Tale retelling itself again and again
until it cannot tell the tale's end
from its beginning: River—as ever,

name for what is not quite itself
today: what's become of snowfields, what's
becoming the tear in the elephant's eye.

Whispered name for that which whispers too
in its inscrutable language, surface
flashing silver, specked

with soaked twigs, drowned gnats,
dragonfly wings. Below the surface,
what's changed or changing: bottle

sunk to its neck in mud, pebbles
concealing the salmon's thousand eggs,
sand proceeding by single grains

to the place it will stiffen to stone.
An ax handle worn smooth, some small thing's
rib, cattle teeth, trifocals

plopped in the drink off a fisherman
bending intently over the swirling deep
to make out God's thread mark. Water

flowing at the speed of half-knowledge,
necessity wrestling with desire,
compelled by its only hunch to move

in one direction, compelled
by the breath of something more
that's passing, that passes without a name.

Against Summer

Too many trees, too much blind
geometry: strict, intricate
twig-work, symmetry

of hickory leaf and nut,
the one-minded plum drawing
light in to round a slim white petal.

I unsettle myself with myself.
In a fever of thought, I've wrung
my thumb from its socket.

Easy leafiness. All this calm
shape-shift, swift blossoming,
long limb lowering itself

for the swollen peach. All this
knuckle and adjust,
this wild reason.

The Garden I'm Given

I tend a garden where nothing grows,
where seeds swell in the thin soil,
shrink, and stiffen into little tombs.

Roses rot in the rain. Exhausted
stems strain to nudge crumbs of dirt
then choke in the open air. Slugs

drop from the high, useless trellis
and dot the ground, oozing and dumb
like lopped-off thumbs.

I furrow and rake, I mulch
and make nothing, but murmur
names as I labor, letting

the delicate syllables settle
and root on the tongue, or bloom
at the back of the teeth:

Tulip. Begonia. Crocus.
Lilac. Bloodroot. Moonflower.
Glory-of-the-snow. In the garden

I'm given, my only plot, I plant,
mangle, and botch, but sing as I do,
it's my work, I dig in, I keep at it.

Notes

The Dostoyevsky epigraph is translated by Henry and Olga Carlisle.

"The New World": The epigraph is from "Passage to India." "By the Bivouac's Fitful Flame" is a Whitman title.

Section II: The Strand epigraph is from *Dark Harbor* IX.

Section III: The Wright epigraph is from "Disjecta Membra," from BLACK ZODIAC.

"As Columbus Would Have It, the Earth Like a Pear": "Dante, it is recalled, had placed Paradise on the summit of the mountain of Purgatory, which his century situated in the middle of an imagined ocean covering the whole of the Southern Hemisphere; and Columbus at first shared this mythological idea. The earth, he wrote, is shaped 'like a pear, of which one part is round, but the other, where the stalk comes, elongated'" (Joseph Campbell, *The Masks of God: Creative Mythology*).

"But Look Where Sadly the Poor Wretch Comes Reading": The title is from *Hamlet*, Act II, Scene ii.

Acknowledgments

Artful Dodge: "Sanctum Sanctorum"

Birmingham Poetry Review: "Absolution," "O.K. Fine," "The Old Sense," "A Sickly Child"

Calliope: "Elegy," "Land Edged by Water"

Cream City Review: "Yes, Well"

Fine Madness: "The Church of the Backyard," "Reprisal," "What Furniture Means"

Greensboro Review: "As Columbus Would Have It, the Earth Like a Pear"

Gulf Coast: "Then Again"

Nebraska Review: "What the Earth Knows"

New Delta Review: "Against Summer"

Plainsongs: "Something or Other"

Prairie Schooner: "Cracking Open," "The Woman Who Could Not Wear a Hat"

Tar River Poetry: "Night Construction"

West Branch: "Panorama without a View"

Willow Springs: "But Look Where Sadly the Poor Wretch Comes Reading," "An Honest Forest," "Without Presumptions"

"River" appeared in the Riverstone Press anthology *Pebbles*

"Night Construction," "Reprisal," "To Faint Forth Tearfully," and "The Workings of the Internal Combustion Engine" also appeared in the anthology *45/96: South Carolina Poetry* published by Ninety-Six Press

Some of these poems first appeared in *Crumbs of Bread*, a chapbook published by March Street Press

For their help, direct or indirect, with the writing of these poems, thanks to the Trident Community Foundation, The Group, and my family—especially my mother, Ange Forhan Scott. First honors always to Kevin Forhan, Alex Kuo, and Charles Simic, leaders by example. Finally, eternal gratitude to Ellen Bryant Voigt, without whom . . .